CHRISTINA ROSSETTI

CHRISTINA ROSSETTI

MARNIE POMEROY

Greenwich Exchange
London

Greenwich Exchange, London

First published in Great Britain in 2020
All rights reserved

Christina Rossetti
© Marnie Pomeroy, 2020

Printed and bound by imprintdigital.com
Cover design by December Publications
Tel: 07951511275

Greenwich Exchange Website: www.greenex.co.uk

Cataloguing in Publication Data is available
from the British Library

ISBN: 978-1-910996-38-6

With thanks to Warren Hope
for encouragement and suggested source material

and to Dr. Ralph Zabel, ophthalmologist,
who kept light on the writing of this

CONTENTS

BIOGRAPHICAL NOTES & CHRONOLOGY

GABRIELE PASQUALE GIUSEPPE ROSSETTI (1783-1854): Christina Rossetti's Roman Catholic father, an Italian poet and writer, who became a political exile from Italy.

FRANCES MARY LAVINIA POLIDORI (1800-1886): Christina's Anglican mother, Italian-English, trained as a governess.

MARIA FRANCESCA ROSSETTI (1827-1876): Christina's sister, a writer, who became a nun.

GABRIEL CHARLES DANTE ROSSETTI, called Dante Gabriel (1828-1882): her brother, a well-known poet, painter, and founder of Pre-Raphaelites.

WILLIAM MICHAEL ROSSETTI (1829-1919): her brother, a writer and critic. He contributed articles to the eleventh edition Encyclopedia Britannica.

CHRISTINA GEORGINA ROSSETTI (5 December 1830-29 December 1894).

1826   Gabriele Rossetti marries Frances Polidori in
            London.

1830   *5 December*: Their fourth child, Christina
            Georgina Rossetti, is born.

1831   Gabriele becomes a professor of Italian at
            King's College London.

1837   Both sons, Dante Gabriel and William, are
            enrolled in King's College School.

1841   Dante Gabriel attends the art academy in
            Bloomsbury, after which he became
            widely known as a poet, illustrator, and painter.

1842   Christina writes her first poem, 'To my Mother
            on her Birthday'.

1843   Christina attends Christ Church under Rev
            William Dodsworth, famed preacher of the
            Oxford Movement (Tractarianism), a Catholic
            revival.

1844   Maria becomes a governess.

1845   William begins working as a clerk at the Inland
            Revenue Board where he stays until 1894.
            During this time he is also an art critic for *The
            Spectator*, a chronicler, and a notable man of
            letters.
            Christina suffers a serious but undefined illness.

1847   Her *Verses, Dedicated to her Mother*, is
privately printed by Gaetano Polidori,
Christina's maternal grandfather.
Her father, having become ill, resigns from
King's College. He begins tutoring private
students, among them Charles Bagot Cayley.

1848   *September*: The Pre-Raphaelite Brotherhood
(PRB) is founded by Dante Gabriel with friends.
October: Christina publishes her first poems.
She becomes engaged to James Collinson,
member of the PRB.

1849   *Spring and summer*: She suffers further
illnesses.

1850   *January*: Two poems by Christina are published
under a pen name by the PRB in their first issue
of *The Germ*, which folds after three more
issues, having printed a total of seven of her
poems.
May: She breaks off her engagement with James
Collinson when he returns to Catholicism.
August: She travels with Maria to Brighton
where she falls ill.
November: The Rossetti family moves to 38
Arlington Street.

1851   Christina and her mother start a day school that
fails a year later.
Dante Gabriel paints Elizabeth Siddal.

1852   Christina and her mother run a school in
            Somerset.

1854   They move back to London, 145 Upper Albany
            Street, to take care of her father.
            April: Gabriele Rossetti dies.
            Autumn: Christina volunteers as a nurse to aid
            the wounded in the Crimean war, but is
            rejected for being inexperienced and too
            young.

1856   William is engaged to Henrietta Rintoul.

1858   *February*: James Collinson marries.

1859   Like her sister, Maria, Christina volunteers her
            services at the St Mary Magdalen Home for
            Fallen Women (possibly until 1870), declining
            to head their organisation when asked.
            27 April: She writes *Goblin Market*.

1860   Her poems and prose begin to be published
            more widely.
            May: Dante Gabriel marries Elizabeth Siddal.
            November: William and Henrietta end their
            engagement.

1861   *June*: Christina travels to France with her
            mother and William.

1862   *February*: Elizabeth Siddal Rossetti dies. (Dante
            Gabriel buries his manuscript of poems in the

coffin with her, but has it retrieved in 1868.)
March: The Rossetti siblings begin helping with
the Gilchrist book on William Blake.
April: *Goblin Market and Other Poems* is
published.

1864   Christina spends three months in Hastings to
        improve her health.

1865   A second edition of *Goblin Market* is
        published.
        She, her mother, and William travel in Europe.

1866   *The Prince's Progress and Other Poems* is
        finished.
        August: Christina rejects Charles Cayley's
        proposal of marriage.

1867   Christina moves to 56 Euston Square in
        Bloomsbury with her mother, Maria, William,
        and two Polidori aunts. (A third aunt dies that
        year.)

1871   Christina is diagnosed with Graves' disease.

1872   *Sing-Song: A Nursery Rhyme Book*, illustrated
        by Arthur Hughes, is published.
        June: Dante Gabriel begins to suffer mental
        illness caused by whisky taken with chloral
        hydrate to control his pain from botched
        surgery.

1873   *July*: William is engaged to Lucy Brown,
              daughter of the painter, Ford Madox Brown.
              September: Maria moves to a convent.

1874   William and Lucy Brown are married.

1875   Publication of: *Goblin Market, The Prince's
              Progress and Other Poems.*
              William and Lucy's first child, Olivia Frances
              Rossetti, is born. (As an adult she becomes a
              friend of Ezra Pound.)

1876   Maria Francesca dies.
              Christina, her mother, and two aunts move
              again within Bloomsbury.
              Christina's poems are published in Boston,
              USA.

1877   William and Lucy's second child, Gabriel
              Arthur Rossetti, is born.

1879   Their third child, Helen Maria Rossetti, is born.

1881   Their twins, Mary Elizabeth and Michael Ford
              Rossetti, are born.
              James Collinson dies.

1882   Christina's *Poems* are published in Boston.
              April: Dante Gabriel dies.

1883   Michael, the son of William and Lucy, dies.
              Charles Bagot Cayley dies.

1886   Frances Polidori Rossetti, Christina's mother, dies.

1890   Christina's *Poems: New and Enlarged Edition* is published in both London and New York.

1892   Christina is diagnosed with breast cancer and undergoes a mastectomy at home.
            After the death of Tennyson, she is thought of as a candidate for Poet Laureate.

1893   *Verses*, her book of devotional poems, published by the Society for the Promotion of Christian Knowledge, is also published in New York.

1894   *April*: Lucy Rossetti dies.
            29 December: Christina Rossetti dies. She is buried in Highgate Cemetery.

1896   *New Poems, Hitherto Unpublished or Uncollected*, is published.

1904   *The Poetical Works of Christina Georgina Rossetti, with Memoir and Notes by William Michael Rossetti,* is published and remains her standard collection for the next seventy-five years.

            On the Anglican Church liturgical calendar, 27 April has been appointed as a feast day to venerate Christina Rossetti.

INTRODUCTION

THE MAGIC OF CHRISTINA ROSSETTI'S POEMS made Sara Teasdale, the well-known American poet, fall in love with poetry as a child. To write Christina's biography late in her too short life, she travelled to England where she became ill and had to return home to America. She died before being able to write the planned work, grievous losses in both respects.

Although Christina Rossetti doesn't spring to mind as one of our major poets, she remains quietly near the top, ready to surprise readers who don't know her poems. Many must be puzzled by her unpegged status when discovering her best ones. Among these, the highly original 'Goblin Market', colourful, spooky, and strange, has attracted interpretation even though she insisted that she had nothing in mind beyond the story itself. 'A Birthday', a short, rich, jubilant lyric, is likely to be familiar because much anthologised, which is also true of the sonnet, 'Remember'. With variety as one of her distinctions, these three differ greatly.

Many of her poems, including selections from her *Sing-Song: A Nursery Rhyme Book* for children, were intended for musical settings such as hymns, and some did become songs or Christmas carols. 'Song' – 'When I am dead, my dearest' (1848) – acquired eleven musical settings, according to Christina's brother, William. Gustav Holst composed music for 'A Christmas Carol', called also 'Bleak Midwinter' (circa 1872). Another, 'Christmastide' (1885), also known as 'Love Came Down at Christmas', inspired many musicians. It was given a modern treatment in 2007 and performed with a new setting in 2014. These are just a few of her poems known through music.

Although she has been familiar through several poems in anthologies, the monumental quantity of Christina's collected work, more recently published, may be daunting. But her variety has urged many selections to be chosen from her work, suggesting that there must be something for everyone, and making *Christina Rossetti: The Complete Poems* (Penguin), over two inches thick, tempting to explore.

Christina speaks simply, and her expert rhyming draws us into the ballads that tell stories, her outbursts in many forms, and whatever mood or situation she wanted to express. Further familiarity should bring her the status she merits.

***

Gabriele Pasquale Giuseppe Rossetti, born in Abruzzo, Italy, was a nobleman, eminent poet, student of Dante, and founder of the secret society, the *Carbonari*. Because for four generations before his birth so many members of his family had red hair, they adopted the nickname 'Rossetti'.

Gabriele had to flee from Italy on account of his Liberal beliefs as a reformer. He finally settled in London, where, in 1826, he married Frances Mary Lavinia Polidori, daughter of another Italian exile. Her brother, Dr Polidori, was the poet Lord Byron's physician.

In 1831, Gabriele became a noted professor of Italian at King's College.

While he was an easygoing Roman Catholic, his wife was a devout Anglican. When they had children, he was responsible for the boys' education, and she, for the home tutoring of the girls.

From earliest childhood, Christina remembered that her father would crow like a cock in the morning to wake them up.

Gabriele had written a book, *The Mystery of the Platonic Love in the Middle Ages*, limited in both its printing and distribution because of the unrespectable subject matter. Upon his death in 1854, Frances burned what copies he had left at home, but because he had given some of them to friends, the work can now be accessed online.

Their eldest daughter, born 1827, was Maria Francesca, later nicknamed 'Moony' for her round face by Christina. She was the author of *Shadow of Dante*, considered an important contribution by Dante scholars, and exceptionally useful by his general readers. During times of family financial troubles, she became a governess, and at one point tutored Lucy Madox Brown, her future sister-in-law, who would marry her brother, William. Christina dedicated *Goblin Market* to her. When young, Maria developed unreciprocated feelings of love for a family friend, the well-known art critic John Ruskin, whose essays are still widely read. At age forty-six she entered a nunnery, dying three years later of ovarian cancer.

Maria's birth was followed in 1828 by that of Gabriele Charles Dante, later called Dante Gabriel – celebrated painter, illustrator, and poet. In 1848, he and some friends founded the Pre-Raphaelite Brotherhood, the PRB, as it came to be known, whose romantic, detailed, intensely coloured art was inspired by love of nature and the medieval. Perhaps because their meetings were held in William Holman Hunt's studio late at night, and Christina was young and shy, she didn't join them, but was nevertheless always associated with the group.

William Michael, born in 1829, became a civil servant and a literary critic and man of letters, who also wrote many articles for the 1911 edition of the *Encyclopaedia Britannica*. While Christina had often shown her poems to both brothers, William left notes for some of them in use today, and we regret not having more. He lived to write the last word about his siblings.

Christina Georgina, the youngest, was born in 1830.

That year was notable for the birth of two extremely prolific, stellar English-speaking women poets: Emily Dickinson in Amherst, Massachusetts, the USA, and Christina Rossetti in London, England.

Many poems may startle the reader within the vast collected works of each. Emily Dickinson wrote 1,789 poems, mostly short with short lines, in forms familiar to her from hymns. Christina Rossetti wrote 1,142 in every form that she could think of. (One must count the first lines in her index, not the titles, because there are sometimes several separate poems under one title.)

Although God is frequently mentioned by Emily Dickinson in a matter-of-fact, or at least in an uncomplicated way, many of Christina's poems have a religious cast with a difference. Sometimes they stop short, somewhat unexpectedly and almost as though with an effort, to conclude in statements about heaven or God. Christina was reminding herself that here was her chosen goal, despite the distractions and earthly longings on our journey towards death. God and an eternity in heaven would reward her for renouncing earthly pleasures and happiness. When assertions like these sometimes feel as if they had been added on, they don't make us question the sincerity of her religious convictions, but they do suggest, at least, that she was struggling to maintain her renunciations.

As they have been since the English language was young, her poems' lilies and roses are literary – symbols, rather than images. They rarely give off perfume. Even so, such instances of the formulaic detract little from the great vigour of her poems.

Just as Emily Dickinson's condensed verses reflected her intense, cloistered life, so Christina's variety of verse forms accompanied an emotional hunger and restlessness in her single status.

Because so many of her poems are about lack of fulfillment, how everything dies, and a sadness for what was missed, some readers have thought she held a death-wish but a death-awareness would be more accurate. Also she knew that love, even if attained, may disappoint or deceive. Energetic appreciation for life itself comes through in the quantity and variety of poems she wrote, despite having death on her mind. This preoccupation was no doubt from poor health, which began in her teens and made her family fear that she would die young. Beyond that, until penicillin was developed, everyone knew how even a simple chill could become deadly, and that childbirth was a woman's equivalent of men going to war.

All the Romantic poets and artists familiar to her would have been an influence. John Keats (1795-1821) was one, whose tragically short lifespan, driven home to us by those dates, is forever painful to think about. Another was the seventeen-year-old Thomas Chatterton, a poet driven to suicide by society's indifference, and the subject of the popular, sensationalist painting, *The Death of Chatterton* (1856).

Christina lived at home, unmarried, to age sixty-four. Happiness within her remarkable family surely included the writing and success of her poems, although they seemed to have never made up for what she missed.

1

BACKGROUND

THE ROMANTIC ERA SEEMED TO BURST like a piñata over the extravagant hair styles on early 1800s' heads. But the classical world of culture had already begun reacting to developments earlier. Large machinery was coming into use. The poor, the maimed, and the abandoned were packed into cities blackened by coal-dust. By 1845, the steam engine widely served Great Britain. In America, in 1862, Emily Dickinson wrote a poem about a train whose 'horrid, hooting stanza' had become part of the landscape where forests were rapidly being cleared away.

To escape what had become ugly, those who were educated solaced themselves with the arts where now the individual could star, and freshened their minds with whatever nature was still left.

In the arts, there was often a hearkening back to medieval times – the Gothic – as a remote setting for what was beautiful, mysterious, or macabre. The old ballad form was revived. Samuel Taylor Coleridge's 'The Rime of the Ancient Mariner', published in *Lyrical Ballads* in 1789, introduced poems that expressed personal feelings simply, as well as dreams and hallucinatory splendours derived from using opium.

In France, in the field of painting, where Jacques-Louis David and Jean-Auguste-Dominique Ingres had perfected those dazzling rivulets of light on satin in their court portraits, Théodore Géricault used similar techniques to depict mayhem smoothly in his 1819 'Raft of the Medusa'. Eugéne Delacroix, as masterful as any at rendering luxurious surfaces, continued the display of melodrama in 'The Death of Sardanapalus' (1827) and 'Liberty Leading the People' (1830), among other paintings. But these were now bold with colour and brushy paint-strokes to be enjoyed for their own sake. Such tactility led to the French Impressionists, the word 'Impressionism' having been first used insultingly to describe paintings by Claude Monet, Pierre-Auguste Renoir, Edgar Degas, and Camille Pissarro in a show held in Paris in 1874.

English landscape painting in the 1800s also underwent a change, thanks largely to John Constable and J.M.W. Turner. Constable's landscapes were full of feeling for knobbly organic life. Turner's seascapes, with their sunsets, developed into unearthly and original works ahead of their time. (Constable, in a letter to his brother in 1836, famously described Turner's atmospheric paintings as being painted as if 'with tinted steam, so evanescent and so airy'.)

'Swagger portraits' had been much in demand in England as in France. Even in the United States, with its imported culture, artists kept props on hand to offer sitters so that they could appear wealthy and influential. Those earlier portraits were idealised versions of individuals before they became examples of Romantic

prominence, and chosen on a democratic basis.

In 1768, Sir Joshua Reynolds, the first president of the Royal Academy of Arts, had promoted the smooth 'Grand Style', but his later brushstrokes loosened, close to becoming ends in themselves. He was mocked as 'Sir Sloshua' in 1848 by the Pre-Raphaelite Brotherhood, whose members preferred the smooth painting techniques in use before Raphael.

Portraits by the Pre-Raphaelites offered something new by illustrating characters from fantasy, often with medieval touches, where the beautiful might also be strange, and yet, along with paintings of nature, were realistic.

An aside: While Gucci has provided contemporary New Yorkers with John Everett Millais's painting, 'Ophelia', on hoodies and totes, an exhibition in the USA's National Gallery of Art showed that Ruskin and other English Pre-Raphaelites, whose paintings toured the USA from 1857 to 1858, had persuaded certain American artists to imitate them as late as 1900, by recording nature precisely down to the last, veined leaf.

While drama in the arts could express horror and death (Géricault and Delacroix), it also invoked awe by revealing the sublime. In the mid-1800s, American painters, influenced by Turner, produced colossal views of mountains that were volcanic or made luminous by weather.

Surging into a personal space in another form of expression, between 1800 and 1824: Ludwig van Beethoven composed nine symphonies. Hector Berlioz, Richard Wagner, Pyotr Ilyich Tchaikovsky, and Johannes Brahms followed, all of them at home with the sublime and the colossal, as well as with yearning and the intimate.

Literature had kept pace. In 1801, inspired by vast North American forests, François-René de Chateaubriand's hugely successful melodramatic novel, *Atala*, appeared in France.

In the United States, Edgar Allen Poe marketed morbid stories and poems with much success before dying, delirious, at age forty in 1849. Ralph Waldo Emerson, lecturer, essayist – and the first translator of Dante's *La Vita Nuova* into English – circulated ideas about the importance of the individual and of nature, as did his friend, Henry David Thoreau. While Emerson is especially identified with Transcendentalism, they both were foremost in the American Romantic movement. (In 1867, Henry Wadsworth Longfellow, educator and poet, translated Dante's *La Divina Comedia*. He became the first American to do so.)

In Britain, John Keats published his greatest poems in 1819 and 1820. Thought to be mad, the visionary poet and artist William Blake, who died in 1872, was to be called a 'glorious luminary' by William Rossetti.

Thanks to Dante Gabriel's inspired purchase of Blake's notebook in a private sale, for a mere ten shillings and sixpence, it was rescued for posterity. Christina encountered this work in 1862, and Blake's short poems may have influenced her *Sing-Song: A Nursery Rhyme Book*.

She would have been familiar also with the poems of Alfred, Lord Tennyson, poet laureate after William Wordsworth, both of whom were publishing during her lifetime, and those of Robert Browning and his wife, Elizabeth Barrett Browning, whom she revered.

Dante Gabriel Rossetti's paintings, which were very successful with his public, are well known. Among his poems lives the memorable couplet: 'Is memory most of miseries the most miserable/Or the one flower of ease in bitterest hell?' His presence, accompanied by charisma and formidable talents, must have lingered in the midst of his family, with which he always stayed in close touch even after moving elsewhere.

Following the death of his wife, he shared a house for a while with some friends, a larksome group, but the pleasures created within their company were soon overshadowed. He needed drugs to help handle pain from surgery gone wrong.

Meanwhile, he kept many pets – one wombat that behaved like the centerpiece for the dining room table; an elephant that was to be taught to wash the windows; a toucan, which would wear a cowboy hat, and was trained to ride a llama; these and more, for which his adoring aunt, Charlotte Polidori, 'loaned' him money. (The earnings from his paintings, once substantial, must have run low.)

Perhaps she was trying to compete with her sister. Aunt Eliza, who had gone to the Crimean war as a nurse with Florence Nightingale, had received a Turkish medal from Queen Victoria. But then, to recommend her, Aunt Charlotte was custodian of her brother John's scandalous diary of Lord Byron's life, and was said to have shown it to her nieces and nephews.

Dante Gabriel's good days were then few. The chloral hydrate for pain relief was washed down by whisky that destroyed his health. He died in 1882.

In this cultural climate during Queen Victoria's reign (1837-1901), Christina was raised and educated by her beloved mother, with emphasis on Dante, Milton, and, conspicuously, the King James Bible. So rich a personal life amid disappointed romances may have helped account for why she remained unmarried.

2

CHRISTINA

AS A HIGH SPIRITED AND STUBBORN child, Christina had temper tantrums, once even ripping her arm open with scissors. Having developed self-discipline, she matured into a charming young woman, remarked upon especially for the 'lovely, spiritual expression of her eyes, and the firmness of the mouth, revealing strength as well as sweetness of character' (from Mackenzie Bell's *Christina Rossetti: A Biographical and Critical Study*, p15). Her happy development must have been in great part thanks to her mother, who was always adored by her children. Having been trained as a governess, surely she was especially understanding of childhood's difficulties, and tolerated much acting out.

At the age of fifteen, Christina became seriously ill with fainting fits, trouble with her heart, anemia, and what was described then as nervous exhaustion. The themes of death and of preferring heaven to earthly pleasures, frequent in her poems, no doubt were connected to these bouts of illness.

At the age of seventeen, Christina was thought to be Dante

Gabriel's first model for his very first painting, a preliminary study for 'The Girlhood of Mary Virgin.' When young, she had been considered beautiful. Thanks to an artist brother with artist friends, many drawings and quite a few paintings exist of her. Some examples: James Collinson, to whom she was later engaged, painted her portrait in oils; Holman Hunt modeled her head in clay; and Christina again sat for the Virgin Mary in her brother's later painting, where she is indeed lovely: 'Ecce Ancilla Domini', best known as 'The Annunciation', hangs at present in the Tate Gallery in London, and is widely reproduced.

We easily recognise the strong features, a rather long jaw, and sad eyes. John R. Clayton, an artist, remarked to Mackenzie Bell (*Christina Rossetti, a Biographical and Critical Study*, p20): '... that it was from the "the fascinating mystery and soft melancholy of his sister's eyes," that Dante Gabriel gained that impulse toward the sad female face so noticeable in the pictorial work of his whole career.'

Her eyes were remarked upon by a friend of Dante Gabriel, Theodore Watts-Dunton, who wrote in *The Antheneum*, 'She had Gabriel's eyes, in which hazel and blue-grey were marvelously blent, one hue shifting into the other, answering to the movements of the thoughts' and 'When a young girl, at the time that she sat for the Virgin ... she was ... really lovely, with an extraordinary expression of pensive sweetness.'

Her voice was also noticed for being especially beautiful – softly musical as she conversed in the Italian language with family, visiting revolutionaries and writers.

Added to English, a rich language, but one that is best spoken with pleasant voices, or else, as has been observed, it seems angry, this would have helped fine-tune her ear, predisposed to enjoying the sounds of words. Already having a talent for versifying, she played the game of *bouts-rimés* with her brothers from an early age, which would have greatly furthered her ease with rhymes. Yet, although she would have liked certain of her poems to be sung as hymns, in keeping with her being very devout, music itself seemed not to have engaged her.

McKenzie Bell's book quotes Henri Jacottet (p167) 'I don't consider that Christina had any dislike of music ... would even say that in a certain sense she liked and admired it – But she had no sort of musical gift of her own.' Bell then wrote 'There was no piano or any musical instrument of any kind in her house, and I never heard her allude in talk in the faintest degree to the pleasure derivable from music.'

While her brother, Dante Gabriel, did make use of musical instruments in his paintings, this was only for their shapes or what they symbolised. One can see that either the positions of the players' hands were wrong for music-making, or objects in the paintings would have obstructed the sound, such as folds of a dress lying across strings.

Nevertheless, Christina is one of our most musical poets. This may have related to her beautiful speaking voice, and to her great talent at versifying, in the way she linked the sounds of words together.

As her aptitude lay in sensitivity to words as sound more than image, she cultivated verse further in the direction of rhymed prose, rather than in poetry, which flares out of a surprise juxtaposition of words. Genius in her work could be said to lie mostly in how she rhymed situations and little stories, gratifying the inner ear. Judging by the amount Christina wrote, she must have made use of almost every actual or potential story she encountered, her ease extending through any verse form.

Perhaps because of supreme confidence as a skilled metrist, she sometimes allowed herself variations in her verse structures and rhyme schemes. The poem 'Christian and Jew. A Dialogue' (1858) exemplifies this: AABBA; AABBB; AABABA; AABBA; ABABA; ABBABB; AABAB; ABABB; ABABB; ABAAB; ABBAB; ABBABB. (The poem is rapturous, so irregularity suits it especially.)

She was also flexible within her subject matter – comfortable with endings sometimes not entirely tidy or quite what you might expect. And she often told stories that stopped while still in an ongoing situation, as does much fiction today. As is true also for other forms of art, poems that are somewhat open-ended resonate far into a lifelike space.

Very many of her poems are religious – personal outbursts that address God. Her older sister, Maria, entered a convent, while Christina rejected two (possibly three) proposals of marriage on religious grounds. She had been engaged to marry James Collinson, and we have to assume that she would have married him if he had not reverted to Roman Catholicism, from which he had lapsed. Her decision is puzzling, since her father was Roman Catholic and her mother High Anglican, with no evident discord.

She renounced a married life that might have been more fulfilling than spinsterhood, even with an adored, interesting mother and two beloved brothers (one endlessly colourful). She seemed to come to have regrets about her choice, ever afterwards trying to convince herself that serving God with heaven at the end was the preferred path.

In 'The Novice' (1847) she wrote:

> Yea, it is as a poison cup
> That holds one quick fire-draught within;
> For when the life seems to begin
>   The slow death looketh up.

Yet, despite this view of romantic love, to commit herself to celibacy appeared to take a continual effort of zeal, reinforced by the picture of how devoted Christians see heaven.

3

SOME POEMS FROM 1847-1856

UP UNTIL CHRISTINA'S NINTH YEAR, WHEN her maternal grandfather lived among orchards and fields, she visited him, and the fruit trees and small animals found there often entered her poems. She never hesitated to hold a frog, toad, or caterpillar in her hand, which later would help write them into life. Although that early time would have given her the fullest contact with the natural world she would ever know, in London she lived near a park long enough to go there for renewal.

Her precise writing about nature shows how sharp was her eye, and how exact her word-sense. Here are two instances from 'Twilight Calm' (1850). In the first example, this tiny, nervous life contrasts in every way with the immense, rooted tree:

> The dormouse squats and eats
> Choice little dainty bits
> Beneath the spreading roots of a broad lime;
> Nibbling his fill he stops from time to time
> And listens where he sits.

In the second, sundown's cooler temperature brings forth insects for the hungry bat; a darkening that the owl can hunt in (its broad eyes – well observed – are blind by day); and dew needed to moisten pathways for slimy slugs. No paraphrasing can bring the scene to life like Christina's poetry:

> The gnats whirl in the air,
> The evening gnats; and there
> The owl opes broad his eyes and wings to sail
> For prey; the bat wakes, and the shell-less snail
> Comes forth, clammy and bare.

From 'When the cows come home ... ' in *Sing-Song: A Nursery Rhyme Book,* (1872) the verb 'winks' is strong and exact:

> And timid, funny, brisk little bunny,
> Winks his nose, and sits all sunny.

And in 'Child's Talk in April' (1855), birds hatching is witnessed first-hand:

> Fancy the breaking of the shell,
> The chirp, the chickens wet and bare ...

One poem from *Sing-Song* is a useful mnemonic for knowing if the moon is waxing or waning:

> O Lady Moon, your horns point toward the east:
> Shine, be increased;
> O Lady Moon, your horns point toward the west:
> Wane, be at rest.

In her seventeenth year, when Christina's grandfather had her poems privately printed, she composed 'The Dead City' (1847), a bad dream in writing.

Christina had lived near Mme Tussaud's waxwork exhibition, and was familiar with the story of 'The Sleeping Beauty', where the entire court slept until the prince kissed the princess awake. In her poem, a pleasant stroll leads through darkness to a bright walled city with a magnificent palace and garden – all deserted – but in a tent on the other side, a lifelike crowd of people of all ages are frozen at a banquet, carpeted by flowers (roses and lilies again).

'Grapes were hanging overhead/Purple, pale, and ruby red', under which ripe fruits compare to those that the goblins had purveyed. The banqueters are stone, but tinted with lifelike colours, and arrested in lifelike acts of feasting.

The poem takes its time to arrive at the banquet. Perhaps the long, varied preamble has significance. Line 164 introduces a hint, when the breezes suggest she enter the tent and see 'How for luxury and pride/a great multitude have died'. The poem ends by setting her straight again: 'What was I that I should see/So much hidden mystery?/And I straightway knelt and prayed' – Christina keeping on her many-years-long path to God.

The end, which leaves the experience baffling to both reader and to Christina, is typical of those in which she sidesteps an anticipated closure, and disappears behind the veil of prayer.

We can only wish that 'A Pause of Thought' (1848) were written dispassionately. This first stanza may describe Christina's single state all too well:

> I looked for that which is not, nor can be,
>   And hope deferred made my heart sick in truth:
>   But years must pass before a hope of youth
>   Is resigned utterly.

She used this poem as the first part in the three-part poem, 'Three Stages', begun in 1848 and completed in 1854. (See 'A Selection of Poems' at the back of this book.) In his note about these poems, her brother William indicated that she withheld parts two and three from publication because they gave away too much of her personal life.

The second line in part 1 – 'And hope deferred made my heart sick in truth' – is an example of the Bible's influence on Christina's poems. (From the King James Version, Proverbs 13:12 – 'Hope deferred maketh the heart sick: but when the desire cometh, it is a tree of life.' Her mother reminded her that the tree of life was the cross, upon which hung mankind's greatest hope.)

A poem that has eleven musical settings, and which may be compared to 'Remember', is 'When I am Dead, my Dearest' (1848):

> When I am dead, my dearest,
> Sing no sad songs for me;
> Plant thou no roses at my head,
> Nor shady cypress tree:
> Be the green grass above me
> With showers and dewdrops wet;
> And if thou wilt, remember,
> And if thou wilt, forget.
>
> I shall not see the shadows,
> I shall not feel the rain;
> I shall not hear the nightingale
> Sing on, as if in pain:
> And dreaming through the twilight
> That doth not rise nor set,
> Haply I may remember,
> And haply may forget.

'Remember' (1849) is widely anthologised and deservedly so. A romantic relationship, seen ending in a physical death to come, is a theme that presents itself to many lovers, and which would be expected of Christina given her cast of mind. The opening is most affecting. Line four depicts a complex motion so clearly that it can be seen and at the same time felt in the reader's body. What it suggests is, by far, more powerful than what can be said:

> Remember me when I am gone away,
>> Gone far away into the silent land;
>> When you can no more hold me by the hand,
> Nor I half turn to go yet turning stay.
> Remember me when no more day by day
>> You tell me of our future that you planned:
>> Only remember me; you understand
> It will be late to counsel then or pray.
> Yet if you should forget me for a while
>> And afterwards remember, do not grieve:
>> For if the darkness and corruption leave
>> A vestige of the thoughts that once I had,
> Better by far you should forget and smile
>> Than that you should remember and be sad.

The sonnet form demands an almost impossible-to-deliver fourteen lines of sustained power, which is all too rare even for our stalwarts. For example, Wordworth's 'On the Extinction of the Venetian Republic' with its brilliant beginning and stirring end, is extended by means of prosaic argument in between. In 'Remember', 'It will be late to counsel then or pray', is the only line that strays from the core message and seems to be inserted for rhyme. Christina's end is as strong and poignant as her beginning.

This poem was written from a generous heart. Although no one can be sure how far any work is autobiographical, here is personal immediacy with movement that is life-sized.

In a ballad, the spooky 'Moonshine' (1852), the lover holds her hand 'Faithful to his pledge,/Guiding the vessel/From the water's edge.' This is another water setting, and another Death-and-the-Maiden theme: '"Love," she saith, weeping,/"Loose thy hold awhile,/"My heart is freezing/In thy freezing smile."' But they continue: 'Onward and onward,/Far across the sea;/Onward and onward,/Pale as pale can be ... '

This contrasts with the end of 'Love from the North', a ballad written four years later, where the abduction is romantically picture-perfect-happy, depending upon interpretation. Had Christina allowed herself to imagine happiness in love in 1856? That was the year her brother, William, was engaged to Henrietta Rintoul. Even though the engagement ended, the couple's frame of mind at the time must have had an effect on her.

The poem 'Portraits' (1853) with its personal note, makes a welcome surprise appearance from a financially chaotic time in Christina's life. She and her mother, having failed at running two schools, were settling into living on what small income was available within the family.

The first stanza describes her younger brother William. There had originally been a middle section that portrayed Dante Gabriel, said to have been torn out by his 'rather arbitrary hand, beyond a doubt' (notes by William, p1122, *Christina Rossetti, The Complete Poems*) – such a pity, as it was certain to have accurately sketched that outsized personality. The end stanza explains her happiness to stay home:

An easy lazy length of limb,
    Dark eyes and features from the south,
A short-legged meditative pipe
    Set in a supercilious mouth:
Ink and a pen and papers laid
    Down on a table for the night,
Beside a semi-dozing man
    Who wakes to go to bed by light.

A pair of brothers brotherly,
    Unlike and yet how much the same
In heart and high-toned intellect,
    In face and bearing, hope and aim:
Friends of the selfsame treasured friends
    And of one home the dear delight,
Beloved of many a loving heart
    And cherished both in mine, good night.

In the same vein, in the section *Unpublished Poems*, there is a
scrap of verse, (1853), about the Pre-Raphaelite Brotherhood,
further proving Christina's sense of fun:

The two Rossettis (brothers they)
And Holman Hunt and John Millais
With Stephens chivalrous and bland,
And Woolner in a distant land,
In these six men I awestruck see
Embodied the great P.R.B.
D.G. Rossetti offered two
Good pictures to the public view:
Unnumbered ones great John Millais,
And Holman more than I can say

William Rossetti calm and solemn
Cuts up his brethren by the column.

The 'two good pictures' offered by D.G. Rossetti were 'The Girlhood of Mary Virgin' (1849) and 'Ecce Ancilla' (1850), in both of which Christina had modelled for Mary. The cutting up of his brethren by the column, by William, refers to his writer self as critic.

Christina was shortly to meet the challenge offered by *The Rime of the Ancient Mariner*, and use imagery similar to Coleridge's in this stanza from her 'Sleep at Sea' (1853):

> So dream the sleepers,
>   Each man in his place;
> The lightning shows the smile
>   Upon each face:
> The ship is driving, driving,
>   It drives apace:
> And sleepers smile, and spirits
>   Bewail their case.

For those with a taste for dream poems, her much later 'A Ballad of Boding' (1881) is another – atypical, eerie, and violent, from a bad time.

'The World' (1854), with some powerful flourishes, gives life to her chosen direction by depicting its opposite. She must have enjoyed creating the monster, a change from roses and lilies. The adjectives in the third line are just noise, not making an image while she makes her case, and the same is true for the banal line six. But then the beast grins, 'in all the naked horror of the truth' (a ringing line), and conviction arrives:

> By day she wooes me, soft, exceeding fair;
> But all night as the moon so changeth she;
> Loathsome and foul with hideous leprosy

And subtle serpents gliding in her hair.
By day she wooes me to the outer air,
Ripe fruits, sweet flowers, and full satiety:
But thro' the night, a beast she grins at me,
A very monster void of love and prayer,
By day she stands a lie: by night she stands
In all the naked horror of the truth
With pushing horns and clawed and clutching hands.
Is this a friend indeed; that I should sell
My soul to her, give her my life and youth,
Till my feet, cloven too, take hold on hell?

The actual sense of some of her poems is sometimes overwhelmed by the sheen of the poetry. The first stanza of 'Echo' (1854) is an example, seductive with musicality helped by the evocative words, *silence, night, dream, tears,* and all the nouns in the last line:

Come to me in the silence of the night;
    Come in the speaking silence of a dream;
Come with soft rounded cheeks and eyes as bright
    As sunlight on a stream;
        Come back in tears,
O memory, hope, love of finished years.

Victorian buzzwords that serve as fillers are *sweet, fair, tender,* and *noble,* which turned up too often throughout the period.

The weird is easy to account for in her poems, especially assuming she had read Coleridge's *The Rime of the Ancient Mariner,* published over fifty years earlier. In 'My Dream' (1855), after an imposing description of fantasy-crocodiles, we have further the stuff of nightmares:

> Then from far off a wingèd vessel came,
> Swift as a swallow, subtle as a flame:
> I know not what it bore of freight or host,
> But white it was as an avenging ghost.
> It leveled strong Euphrates in its course ...

The silent, unnatural speed of this white ship with wings makes it terrifying.

Dante Gabriel criticised 'The Lowest Room' (1856) for its 'taint' of 'modern vicious style' and 'falsetto muscularity' (notes by William, p934, *Christina Rossetti, The Complete Poems*), but Christina ignored him. Its many strong passages describe scenes from the *Iliad*. Here is one:

> Crest-rearing kings with whistling spears;
> 　　But if these shivered in the shock,
> They wrenched up hundred-rooted trees,
> 　　Or hurled the effacing rock.

One form with variations Christina made frequent use of to tell a tale was the ballad. (Her mother was said to be a great storyteller, making this natural for her.) And in 1856 she also wrote 'Love From the North':

> I had a love in soft south land,
> 　　Beloved through April far in May;
> He waited on my lightest breath,
> 　　And never dared to say me nay.
>
> He saddened if my cheer was sad,
> 　　But gay he grew if I was gay;
> We never differed on a hair,
> 　　My yes his yes, my nay his nay.

The wedding hour was come, the aisles
    Were flushed with sun and flowers that day;
I pacing balanced in my thoughts:
    'It's quite too late to think of nay.' –

My bridegroom answered in his turn,
    Myself had almost answered 'yea':
When through the flashing nave I heard
    A struggle and resounding 'nay'.

Bridesmaids and bridegroom shrank in fear,
    But I stood high who stood at bay:
'And if I answer yea, fair Sir,
    What man art thou to bar with nay?'

He was a strong man from the north,
    Light-locked, with eyes of dangerous grey:
'Put yea by for another time
    In which I will not say thee nay.'

He took me in his strong white arms,
    He bore me on his horse away
O'er crag, morass, and hairbreadth pass,
    But never asked me yea or nay.

He made me fast with book and bell,
    With links of love he makes me stay;
Till now I've neither heart nor power
    Nor will nor wish to say him nay.

'The aisles/were flushed with sun and flowers that day': a solemn, austere place becomes gorgeous for the occasion and all the more fitting for a surprise deliverance. 'Flashing nave' may refer to swords drawn within the commotion.

The adjective *dangerous* in the line ' ... with eyes of dangerous grey' is the spice, the key word, making this man at once exciting ... mysterious ... irresistible, as he interrupts a wedding in which the bride feels trapped. This is the moment arrived at when she must feel especially so, about to commit herself with the pledge, 'I do'. With dignity and spirit, she proves herself equal to the situation by standing up to the intruder.

Later, her lover made her fast 'with book and bell', meaning that she will have been excommunicated by entering into a marriage outside of the church – a compromised, cursed situation. As she is therefore bound to him by default, we might uneasily wonder how her life might go in the years to come, were it not for 'With links of love he makes me stay'. Her having 'neither heart nor power' does not mean beaten down by captivity, but being greatly and enduringly love-struck. The last two lines present a fairy-tale ending despite any Demon Lover overtones.

Christina uses only one rhyme-sound throughout in the most natural way, thus drawing together the oppositions and distances covered. A happily ending love poem, it shows that she understood very well the menace, danger, and importance of sexuality.

4

SOME POEMS FROM 1857-1864

IN 'AN APPLE-GATHERING' (1857), A GIRL walking home from an orchard, empty-handed and alone, was learning several life lessons at the same time:

> I plucked pink blossoms from mine apple tree
> And wore them all that evening in my hair:
> Then in due season when I went to see
> I found no apples there.

While the other girls passed her 'in ones and twos and groups', the sight of their full baskets, and the boyfriends who carried them, mocked her: Willie now was helping plump Gertrude – he, who had once 'stooped to talk' to her, 'Laughing and listening in this very lane' – he, for whom she had adorned her hair with apple blossoms, 'Counting rosiest apples on the earth/Of far less worth than love'. Now, while the others hastened in the chilly evening, she, in her new understanding, ' ... loitered, while the dews/Fell fast I loitered still.'

Aside from what Christina learned at home and from society, her volunteer work at St Mary Magdalen Home for Fallen Women would have yielded much stark, grievous material for narratives. In the poem 'Introspective' (1857), almost unbearably painful to read, stanza fourteen makes use of the Rossetti family motto: *'Frangas non Flectes'* ('I may be broken, but not bent'). This is referred to in the second line, stanza two:

> I wish it were over the terrible pain,
> Pang after pang again and again;
> First the shattering ruining blow,
> Then the probing steady and slow.
>
> Did I wince? I did not faint:
> My soul broke but was not bent;
> Up I stand like a blasted tree
> By the shore of the shivering sea.
>
> On my boughs neither leaf nor fruit,
> No sap in my uttermost root,
> Brooding in an anguish dumb
> On the short past and the long to come.
>
> Dumb I was when the ruin fell,
> Dumb I remain and will never tell:
> O my soul I talk with thee
> But not another the sight must see.
>
> I did not start when the torture stung,
> I did not faint when the torture wrung;
> Let it come tenfold if come it must
> But I will not groan when I bite the dust.

(Note that 'bite the dust', which jars upon our modern ears in this context, probably originated in 1750 with the poet and novelist Tobias Smollett.)

The poem, 'The heart knoweth its own bitterness' (1857) is accompanied by her brother William's note (Christina Rossetti's *The Complete Poems*, pp1136-7): 'Few things written by Christina contain more of her innermost self than this.' Her position, laid out, is direct and tough. 'Deep must call deep until the end', indeed! If instances of Victorian diction and Biblical references were overlooked, she could be speaking in the tone of an awe-inspiring woman today.

> When all the over-work of life
> Is finished once, and fast asleep
> We swerve no more beneath the knife
> But taste that silence cool and deep;
> Forgetful of the highways rough,
> Forgetful of the thorny scourge,
> Forgetful of the tossing surge,
> Then shall we find it is enough?
>
> How can we say 'enough' on earth –
> 'Enough' with such a craving heart?
> I have not found it since my birth,
> But still have bartered part for part.
> I have not held and hugged the whole,
> But paid the old to gain the new:
> Much have I paid, yet much is due,
> Till I am beggared sense and soul.
>
> I used to labour, used to strive
> For pleasure with a restless will:
> Now if I save my soul alive
> All else what matters, good or ill?

I used to dream alone, to plan
    Unspoken hopes and days to come: –
    Of all my past this is the sum –
I will not lean on child of man.

To give, to give, not to receive!
    I long to pour myself, my soul,
Not to keep back or count or leave,
    But king with king to give the whole.
I long for one to stir my deep –
    I have had enough of help and gift –
    I long for one to search and sift
Myself, to take myself and keep.

You scratch my surface with your pin,
    You stroke me smooth with hushing breath: –
Nay pierce, nay probe, nay dig within,
    Probe my quick core and sound my depth.
You call me with a puny call,
    You talk, you smile, you nothing do:
    How should I spend my heart on you,
My heart that so outweighs you all?

Your vessels are by much too strait:
    Were I to pour, you could not hold. –
Bear with me: I must bear to wait,
    A fountain sealed through heat and cold.
Bear with me days or months or years:
    Deep must call deep until the end
    When friend shall no more envy friend
Nor vex his friend at unawares.

Not in this world of hope deferred,
    This world of perishable stuff: –

Eye hath not seen nor ear hath heard
  Nor heart conceived that full 'enough':
Here moans the separating sea,
  Here harvests fail, here breaks the heart:
  There God shall join and no man part,
I full of Christ and Christ of me.

'A Coast-Nightmare' (1857) is creepy and atmospheric, with no escaping to God. It begins:

I have a friend in ghostland –
  Early found, ah me, how early lost! –
Blood-red seaweeds drip along that coastland
  By the strong sea wrenched and tossed ...

Passages continue:

Indistinguished hazy ghosts abound there;
  Troops, yea swarms, of dead men's souls.

and:

They are ghastly men those ghostly freemen:
  Such a sight may you not see. –

The poem ends:

How know you that your lover
  Of death's tideless waters stoops to drink? –
Me by night doth mouldy darkness cover,
  It makes me quake to think:
All night long I feel his presence hover
  Thro' the darkness black as ink.

Without a voice he tells me
  The wordless secrets of death's deep:

> If I sleep, his trumpet voice compels me
>   To stalk forth in my sleep:
> If I wake, he hunts me like a nightmare;
>   I feel my hair stand up, my body creep:
> Without light I see a blasting sight there,
>   See a secret I must keep.

Whatever the interpretations, the poem can be taken as a word-picture of a twilit landscape full of ghosts, an image whose mystery may intrigue the reader most of all. Pictures were part of Christina's mental makeup; she was not Dante Gabriel's sister for nothing.

Both stanzas of 'A Birthday' (1857) are colourful and joyous, and we are glad for Christina, for whom such celebratory feelings were all too rare:

> My heart is like a singing bird
>   Whose nest is in a watered shoot;
> My heart is like an apple-tree
>   Whose boughs are bent with thickset fruit;
> My heart is like a rainbow shell
>   That paddles in a halcyon sea;
> My heart is gladder than all these
>   Because my love is come to me.
>
> Raise me a dais of silk and down;
>   Hang it with vair and purple dyes;
> Carve it in doves and pomegranates,
>   And peacocks with a hundred eyes;
> Work it in gold and silver grapes,
>   In leaves and silver fleurs-de-lys;
> Because the birthday of my life
>   Is come, my love is come to me.

The set of images in the first stanza come from the summer outdoors, while those in the second elaborate upon interior art, Keatsian in rich detail. (Christopher Marlowe's 'Infinite riches in a little room' from *The Jew of Malta* comes to mind.) One might wonder if Christina knew of a piece of furniture, whose gorgeous tactile carvings and inlays fitted together in the enclosed space of a canopied dais or bed; or if the poem was made up of three separate pieces of description that had as yet no rightful home.

Although the two stanzas don't fit perfectly together in a unit, the character of each being different, they connect solidly by means of the last two lines: 'Because the birthday of my life/Is come, my love is come to me.' This poem has often been chosen by anthologists to represent Christina Rossetti.

The greater part of 'Advent' (1858) was set to music for Christina's funeral. Again eight lines to the stanza, it nearly sings itself in a simple meter:

> This Advent moon shines cold and clear,
> These Advent nights are long.
> Our lamps have burned year after year
> And still their flame is strong.

The end: 'Then He shall say, "Arise, My love,/My fair one, come away."' (See 'A Selection of Poems'.)

In 'At Home' (1858), Christina returns as a ghost to her friends celebrating happy future plans. With 'pushed the wine', the gesture is made three-dimensional with 'pushed' – the bottle rasping on the table's top as it makes the rounds. And, as in *Goblin Market*, fruit is all but shared, here in onomatopoeiac succulence – 'sucked the pulp of plum and peach':

> From hand to hand they pushed the wine,
>   They sucked the pulp of plum and peach;
> They sang, they jested, and they laughed,
>   For each was loved of each.

Wrapped up in their full-blown jollity, these friends never think of the spirit who 'all-forgotten, shivered, sad' ... 'who from love had passed away'. At age twenty-eight, Christina *knew*.

'Up-Hill' (1858) is said to be Christina's first poem that caused a stir, so much so that Vincent Van Gogh knew it and used the first stanza in a sermon when he was a young preacher:

> Does the road wind uphill all the way?
>   Yes, to the very end.
> Will the day's journey take the whole long day?
>   From morn to night, my friend.
>
> But is there for the night a resting-place?
>   A roof for when the slow dark hours begin.
> May not the darkness hide it from my face?
>   You cannot miss that inn.
>
> Shall I meet other wayfarers at night?
>   Those who have gone before.
> Then must I knock, or call when just in sight?
>   They will not keep you standing at that door.
>
> Shall I find comfort, travel-sore and weak?
>   Of labour you shall find the sum.
> Will there be beds for me and all who seek?
>   Yea, beds for all who come.

The traveller, who asks the questions, is answered by another with only mortality in mind. His bleak answers make the reader shudder.

Because the poem reads so smoothly, it may not be evident right away that many lines have an irregular number of beats.

Christina showed her poems to both of her brothers for their suggestions. In the case of *Goblin Market* (1859), Dante Gabriel thought up the title, and William later left useful notes, as with many of her other poems in later editions.)

The young Christina's first collection of poems began with *Goblin Market.* She made no effort to regularise its chosen stanza forms, but left them spontaneous and wayward. As she was talented both in writing and drawing, she illustrated the original 1859 version with her watercolours. The 1862 publication was illustrated by Arthur Rackham, with his trademark flare for depicting gnarled woodlands.

In her book, *Sexual Personae*, Camille Paglia's pithy aside – 'Like Christina Rossetti's strange dream-poem *Goblin Market* ... with its embowered sister-sensuality and lush, fruity dangers ... ' – nicely sums it up. This poem is a *tour de force*. Its setting is the goblin-haunted wood next to a farm run by two sisters. To begin:

> Morning and evening
> Maids heard the goblins cry:
> 'Come buy our orchard fruits,
> Come buy, come buy ... '

Christina's exuberant images are their most tactile here, the many kinds of fruit with their luscious, baneful essences mostly in list form. There are 'plump unpecked cherries' and 'figs that fill your mouth' that suggest perfect mouthfeel. Colour and fuzz are palpable to eye, hand, and lip on the 'bloom-down-cheeked peaches', while 'Melons icy-cold' and 'pellucid grapes without one seed' present texture to the imagination. All this ripe fruit weighs down basket, plate, and heavy gold dish, awkwardly hauled and lugged by the goblins.

The goblins themselves come greatly alive with a cat's face, a whisking tail, rats' feet, one crawling like a snail, the clumsy, furry wombat, the tumbling ratel, and one goblin like a parrot … all with sly, leering faces, cooing and whistling and calling in their roles as salesmen. They hobble, tumble, fly, run, leap, puff and blow, chuckle, clap, crow, cluck, and gobble. Later they grunt and snarl, jostle, claw, bark, mew, hiss, and mock. When they disappear, they writhe into the ground, dive into the brook, scud on the gale, or just vanish into the distance – authentic enough to leave a scent of animal musk on the woodland air.

In contrast, the girls are blonde, their chins and fingers are dimpled, and much is made of their white skin and the shining gold of their hair. When sleeping, they are 'Golden head by golden head,/Like two pigeons in one nest/Folded in each other's wings'.

The goblin fruit juices, lethal or later restorative, drip while becoming sticky on the skin:

> But laughed in heart to feel the drip
> Of juice that syrupped all her face,
> And lodged in dimples of her chin,
> And streaked her neck which quaked like curd.

Hints of LGBTQ authority loom over us with interpretations of lesbianism in the lines beginning:

Hug me, kiss me, suck my juices
Squeezed from the goblin fruits for you,
Goblin pulp and goblin dew.
Eat me, drink me, love me;
Laura, make much of me ...

Kissed and kissed and kissed her ...

She kissed and kissed her with a hungry mouth.

The situation is desperate. With each kiss, Laura ingests the life-saving juice, and after the line, 'Her lips began to scorch,' she has to undergo cleansing in various terrifying ways:

Writhing as one possessed she leapt and sung ...

Her locks streamed like the torch
Borne by a racer at full speed ...

Like the watch-tower of a town
Which an earthquake shatters down,
Like a lightning-stricken mast,
Like a wind-uprooted tree
Spun about,
Like a foam-topped waterspout
Cast down headlong in the sea,
She fell at last ...

Thanks to Lizzie's care all through the night, as she hovered over each stirring of pulse and breath, Laura survived her crisis. The story may suggest sexual themes, but also is about sisterly love, with one girl challenging mysterious dangers in order to save the other.

Not all sisters are like them, though. In the poem 'Noble Sisters', one professes the best of motives while she actually sabotages the other's chances for romance and happiness. In 'Sister Maude', Maude's spying and tattling brings about the death of her sister's lover. But those are short poems, and the block-buster *Goblin Market*, with its happy ending, is the standout.

For L.E.L., William said in a footnote that the title referred to a poem by Elizabeth Barrett Browning, which contained the phrase 'thirsty for a little love'. There are echoes from the Bible here (2 Kings and Isaiah) in line three, 'I turn my face in silence to the wall.'

She had originally left lines one and three of each stanza unrhymed, but later Dante Gabriel wrote in rhymes, 'with a brotherly request that I would use them', according to Christina's pencilled-in note in the manuscript notebook, with another further on that added, 'greatly improving the piece ... '

L.E.L. (1859)

Downstairs I laugh, I sport and jest with all:
> But in my solitary room above
I turn my face in silence to the wall;
> My heart is breaking for a little love.
>> Tho' winter frosts are done,
>> And birds pair every one,
And leaves peep out, for springtide is begun.

I feel no spring, while spring is wellnigh blown,
> I find no nest, while nests are in the grove:
Woe's me for mine own heart that dwells alone,
> My heart that breaketh for a little love.
>> While golden in the sun

Rivulets rise and run,
While lilies bud, for springtide is begun.

All love, are loved, save only I; their hearts
        Beat warm with love and joy, beat full thereof:
They cannot guess, who play the pleasant parts,
        My heart is breaking for a little love.
                While beehives wake and whirr,
                And rabbit thins his fur,
In living spring that sets the world astir.

I deck myself with silks and jewelry,
        I plume myself like any mated dove:
They praise my rustling show, and never see
        My heart is breaking for a little love.
                While sprouts green lavender
                With rosemary and myrrh,
For in quick spring the sap is all astir.

Perhaps some saints in glory guess the truth,
        Perhaps some angels read it as they move,
And cry one to another full of ruth,
        'Her heart is breaking for a little love.'
                Tho' other things have birth,
                And leap and sing for mirth,
When spring-time wakes and clothes and feeds the earth.

Yet saith a saint: 'Take patience for thy scathe;'
        Yet saith an angel: 'Wait, for thou shalt prove
True best is last, true life is born of death,
        O thou, heart-broken for a little love.
                Then love shall fill thy girth,
                And love make fat thy dearth,
When new spring builds new heaven and clean new earth.'

'Old and New Year Ditties', number 3, (1860), was said by William Rossetti to be:

> ... the summit and mountain top of Christina's work ... (*Christina Rossetti: The Complete Poems* [Penguin], p912) The poem depends for its effect on nought save its feeling, sense, and sound; for the verses avoid regularity of the ordinary kind, and there is but one single rhyme throughout. The note is essentially one of triumph, though of triumph through the very grievousness of experience past and present.

He added that it was the only poem Christina wrote between 24 July 1860 and 23 March 1861 – about eight months. Hypnotic in sound, it should be read aloud:

> Passing away, saith the World, passing away:
> Chances, beauty and youth, sapped day by day:
> Thy life never continueth in one stay.
> Is the eye waxen dim, is the dark hair changing to grey
> That hath won neither laurel nor bay?
> I shall clothe myself in Spring and bud in May:
> Thou, root-stricken, shalt not rebuild thy decay
> On my bosom for aye.
> Then I answered: Yea.
>
> Passing away, saith my Soul, passing away:
> With its burden of fear and hope, of labour and play,
> Hearken what the past doth witness and say:
> Rust in thy gold, a moth is in thine array,
> A canker is in thy bud, thy leaf must decay.
> At midnight, at cockcrow, at morning, one certain day
> Lo, the Bridegroom shall come and shall not delay:
> Watch thou and pray.
> Then I answered: Yea.

Passing away, saith my God, passing away:
Winter passeth after the long delay:
New grapes on the vine, new figs on the tender spray,
Turtle calleth turtle in Heaven's May.
Tho' I tarry, wait for Me, trust Me, watch and pray.
Arise, come away, night is past and lo it is day,
My love, My sister, My spouse, thou shalt hear Me say.
Then I answered: Yea.

Over and over again, Christina prepared herself to renounce the joys of being alive for the sake of a happiness she hoped to attain after death.

In 'Maude Clare', the second, much shorter version (1862), the queenly wedding guest of that name announces scornfully to the bridegroom that the wedding gifts she brings are her old flame's fickle heart and his paltry love. When Christina cut the poem, drama would make up for what was lost. The mother-in-law-approved bride's answer is hurt and wishful:

'Yea, tho' you're taller by the head,
More wise and much more fair;
I'll love him till he loves me best,
Me best of all, Maude Clare.'

Although the poem stops, the situation does not. We continue to worry about how the rest of the day and the rest of each lifetime shall go for the protagonists. We must pity the determined young bride, faced with the remnants of a passion beyond her domesticated scope.

Some poems attain extra prominence by association. Said to have been one of Christina's favourites, the long, happy, romantic 'Maiden-Song' (1863) is a three-sister-poem with a fairy tale beginning. It was repeated by heart before social gatherings by the Prime Minister of England, William Gladstone:

> Long ago and long ago
>   And long ago still,
> There dwelt three merry maidens
>   Upon a distant hill.
> One was tall Meggan,
>   And one was dainty May,
> But one was fair Margaret,
>   More fair than I can say,
> Long ago and long ago.

Christina made good use of the dynamics of sisterly relations. In stanzas of varying lengths, and in language sometimes mock-extravagant, the story tells how Meggan and May carefully distance themselves from Margaret when they go forth, because they are 'The loveliest maidens near or far/when Margaret was away.' Each sister finds love by singing, which attracts to Meggan a herdsman, to May a shepherd – and to beautiful Margaret, waiting for them by the garden gate and singing with the most ravishing voice, a passerby king:

> Waiting thus in weariness
>   She marked the nightingale
> Telling, if any one would heed,
>   Its old complaining tale.
> Then lifted she her voice and sang,
>   Answering the bird:
> Then lifted she her voice and sang,
>   Such notes were never heard
> From any bird when Spring's in blow.

The king of all that country
    Coursing far, coursing near,
Curbed his amber-bitted steed,
    Coursed amain to hear;
All his princes in his train,
    Squire, and knight, and peer,
With his crown upon his head,
    His sceptre in his hand,
Down he fell at Margaret's knees
    Lord king of all that land,
To her highness bending low.

At the very end:

Sang a golden-bearded king
    Straightway to her feet,
Sang him silent where he knelt
    In eager anguish sweet.
But when the clear voice died away,
    When longest echoes died,
He stood up like a royal man
    And claimed her for his bride.
So three maids were wooed and won
    In a brief May-tide,
Long ago and long ago.

'Songs in a Cornfield' (1864) was set to music as a cantata. Christina had said that it was one of her favourites, and was especially pleased that the poet and critic Algernon Swinburne had praised it. Again, the theme is the lover who comes too late, as in 'The Prince's Progress':

A song in a cornfield
    Where corn begins to fall,

Where reapers are reaping,
 Reaping one, reaping all.
Sing pretty Lettice,
 Sing Rachel, sing May;
Only Marian cannot sing
 While her sweetheart's away.

Where is he gone to
 And why does he stay?
He came across the green sea
 But for a day,
Across the deep green sea
 To help with the hay.
His hair was curly yellow
 And his eyes were grey,
He laughed a merry laugh
 And said a sweet say.

The end:

If he comes to-day
 He will find her weeping;
If he comes to-morrow
 He will find her sleeping;
If he comes the next day
 He'll not find her at all,
He may tear his curling hair,
 Beat his breast and call.

5

SOME POEMS TO 1885

CHRISTINA WROTE MANY SONNETS THAT ARE varied and nuanced. When compared with Gerard Manley Hopkins' sonnet, 'No worst there is none, pitched past pitch of grief', this next one illustrates how Christina's deft rhymes and suave metrics run in the direction of prose, the words perfectly chosen and visceral in their force, but without the transcendence of: 'O the mind, mind has mountains, cliffs of fall/Frightful, sheer, no-man-fathomed.'

Yet her poem, 'Something this foggy day … ' (dated between 1860 and 1884), though not anguished like Hopkins', has power in its direct, craggy, irregular sonnet personality, and ends with almost a wry smile:

> Something this foggy day, a something which
> Is neither of this fog nor of today,
> Has set me dreaming of the winds that play
> Past certain cliffs, along one certain beach,
> And turn the topmost edge of waves to spray:
> Ah pleasant pebbly strand so far away,

So out of reach while quite within my reach,
As out of reach as India or Cathay!
I am sick of where I am and where I am not,
I am sick of foresight and of memory,
I am sick of all I have and all I see,
I am sick of self, and there is nothing new;
Oh weary impatient patience of my lot! –
Thus with myself: how fares it, Friends, with you?

Of Christina's many unique poems, one is 'Cannot Sweeten' (1866), whose title refers to Lady Macbeth in her sleepwalking scene. If a throb of real guilt could have impelled the writing of this, not just Christina's being spellbound by a red and black image, it would be so because of the poem's power:

If that's water you wash your hands in
    Why is it black as ink is black? –
Because my hands are foul with my folly:
    Oh the lost time that comes not back! –

If that's water you bathe your feet in
    Why is it red as wine is red? –
Because my feet sought blood in their goings;
    Red red is the track they tread. –

Slew you mother or slew you father
    That your foulness passeth not by? –
Not father and oh not mother:
    I slew my love with an evil eye. –

Slew you sister or slew you brother
    That in peace you have not a part? –
Not brother and oh not sister:
    I slew my love with a hardened heart.

He loved me because he loved me,
  Not for grace or beauty I had;
He loved me because he loved me;
  For his loving me I was glad.

Yet I loved him not for his loving
  While I played with his love and truth,
Not loving him for his loving,
  Wasting his joy, wasting his youth.

I ate his life as a banquet,
  I drank his life as new wine,
I fattened upon his leanness,
  Mine to flourish and his to pine.

So his life fled as running water,
  So it perished as water spilt:
If black my hands and my feet as scarlet,
  Blacker redder my heart of guilt.

Cold as a stone, as hard, as heavy;
  All my sighs ease it no whit,
All my tears make it no cleaner
  Dropping dropping dropping on it.

This next sonnet is from 'Of My Life' (1866), a sequence containing five poems in various verse forms. Her brother, William, unsympathetic to its drama and melodrama, and not acknowledging the poetry of the end, dismissed the following as a 'morbid effusion' of one of her younger works (from Mackenie Bell's *Christina Rossetti: A Biographical and Critical Study*, p1145). Although one might question parts, and 'rife/With sleep' is an incongruous pairing of words, we are the richer for it:

Yes, I too could face death and never shrink:
But it is harder to bear hated life;
To strive with hands and knees, weary of strife;
    To drag the heavy chain whose every link
    Galls to the bone; to stand upon the brink
Of the deep grave, nor drowse, though it be rife
With sleep; to hold with steady hand the knife
    Nor strike home: this is courage as I think.
Surely to suffer is more than to do:
    To do is quickly done; to suffer is
    Longer and fuller of heart-sicknesses:
    Each day's experience testifies of this:
        Good deeds are many, but good lives are few;
        Thousands taste the full cup; who drains the lees? –

Proof of Christina's sense of fun lies in what was whimsically intended as a lopsided sonnet, also from 'Of My Life' and next in that sequence:

Would that I were a turnip white,
Or raven black,
Or miserable hack
    Dragging a cab from left to right;
    Or would I were the showman of a sight,
Or weary donkey with a laden back,
Or racer in a sack,
    Or freezing traveller on an Alpine height;
Or would I were straw catching as I drown,
        (A wretched landsman I who cannot swim,)
    Or watching a lone vessel sink,
    Rather than writing: I would change my pink
Gauze for a hideous yellow satin gown
        With deep-cut scolloped edges and a rim.

The last in the sequence is this – a sonnet, strictly speaking, though slightly irregular as to rhyme: (a clarence is a four-wheeled carriage that seats four within. The 'Bason' is the basin in St James' Park).

Some ladies dress in muslin full and white,
Some gentlemen in cloth succinct and black;
Some patronise a dog-cart, some a hack,
    Some think a painted clarence only right.
    Youth is not always such a pleasing sight,
Witness a man with tassels on his back;
Or woman in a great-coat like a sack
    Towering above her sex with horrid height.
If all the world were water fit to drown
    There are some whom you would not teach to swim,
    Rather enjoying if you saw them sink;
    Certain old ladies dressed in girlish pink,
With roses and geraniums on their gown: –
    Go to the Bason, poke them o'er the rim.

Written as late as 1885 or 1886, 'Then I Commended Mirth' shows that Christina still looked for enjoyment. (The title is taken from Ecclesiastes 8:15, and the first line from Proverbs 15:15.) Line seven provides the surprise of poetry:

'Then I commended Mirth.'

'A merry heart is a continual feast.'
    Then take we life and all things in good part:
To fast grows festive while we keep at least
    A merry heart

    Well pleased with nature and well pleased with art;
A merry heart makes cheer for man and beast,
    And fancies music in a creaking cart.

> Some day, a restful heart whose toils have ceased,
>   A heavenly heart gone home from earthly mart:
> Today, blow wind from west or wind from east,
>   A merry heart.

During the last period of Christina's life there were many deaths. In 1881, James Collinson died; the next year, Dante Gabriel; the following year, one of the twins born to William and Lucy (Michael Ford, two years old), and also Charles Bagot Cayley. Then, in 1886, her mother.

Part two of the poem, 'Faint, yet Pursuing', consists of a sonnet and four separate short poems related only by Christina's devotion to God. The following irregular triplet was written two years before her death. Uncharacteristically, she didn't regularise it, and in this compact utterance transcended rhyming as she achieved sublime poetry:

> O Lord, I cannot plead my love of Thee:
> I plead Thy love of me; –
> The shallow conduit hails the unfathomed sea.

In that year, 1892, she had a mastectomy – performed in her own home, to treat her breast cancer that was to return.

Lucy Rossetti, William's wife, predeceased her by eight months in 1894. Christina was then suffering acutely before her own death in December, and without the support of so many dear family members and friends. One can only hope that religion served this woman of genius, who shared with us her life's brilliant interior.

A SELECTION OF POEMS

SYMBOLS (1849)

I watched a rosebud very long
    Brought on by dew and sun and shower,
    Waiting to see the perfect flower:
Then, when I thought it should be strong,
    It opened at the matin hour
        And fell at evensong.

I watched a nest from day to day,
    A green nest full of pleasant shade,
    Wherein three speckled eggs were laid:
But when they should have hatched in May,
    The two old birds had grown afraid
        Or tired, and flew away.

Then in my wrath I broke the bough
    That I had tended so with care,
    Hoping its scent should fill the air;
I crushed the eggs, not heeding how
    Their ancient promise had been fair:
        I would have vengeance now.

But the dead branch spoke from the sod,
    And the eggs answered me again:
    Because we failed dost thou complain?
Is thy wrath just? And what if God,
    Who waiteth for thy fruits in vain,
        Should also take the rod?

CONSIDER THE LILIES OF THE FIELD (1853)

Flowers preach to us if we will hear: –
The rose saith in the dewy morn:
I am most fair;
Yet all my loveliness is born
Upon a thorn.
The poppy saith amid the corn:
Let but my scarlet head appear
And I am held in scorn;
Yet juice of subtle virtue lies
Within my cup of curious dyes.
The lilies say: Behold how we
Preach without words of purity.
The violets whisper from the shade
Which their own leaves have made:
Men scent our fragrance on the air,
Yet take no heed
Of humble lessons we would read.

But not alone the fairest flowers:
The merest grass
Along the roadside where we pass,
Lichen and moss and sturdy weed,
Tell of His love who sends the dew,
The rain and sunshine too,
To nourish one small seed.

THREE STAGES

1 (1848)

(first known as 'A Pause of Thought')

I looked for that which is not, nor can be,
 And hope deferred made my heart sick in truth;
 But years must pass before a hope of youth
  Is resigned utterly.

I watched and waited with a steadfast will:
 And thought the object seemed to flee away
 That I so longed for; ever, day by day,
  I watched and waited still.

Sometimes I said: This thing shall be no more:
 My expectation wearies and shall cease;
 I will resign it now and be at peace: –
  Yet never gave it o'er.

Sometimes I said: It is an empty name
 I long for; to a name why should I give
 The peace of all the days I have to live? –
  Yet gave it all the same.

Alas, thou foolish one! alike unfit
 For healthy joy and salutary pain;
 Thou knowest the chase useless, and again
  Turnest to follow it.

2 (1849)

My happy happy dream is finished with,
    My dream in which alone I lived so long.
My heart slept – woe is me, it wakeneth;
    Was weak – I thought it strong.

Oh weary wakening from a life-true dream:
    Oh pleasant dream from which I wake in pain:
I rested all my trust on things that seem,
    And all my trust is vain.

I must pull down my palace that I built,
    Dig up the pleasure-gardens of my soul;
Must change my laughter to sad tears for guilt,
    My freedom to control.

Now all the cherished secrets of my heart,
    Now all my hidden hopes are turned to sin:
Part of my life is dead, part sick, and part
    Is all on fire within.

The fruitless thought of what I might have been
    Haunting me ever will not let me rest:
A cold north wind has withered all my green,
    My sun is in the west.

But where my palace stood, with the same stone,
    I will uprear a shady hermitage;

And there my spirit shall keep house alone,
    Accomplishing its age:

There other garden beds shall lie around
    Full of sweet-briar and incense-bearing thyme;
There I will sit, and listen for the sound
    Of the last lingering chime.

3 (1854)

I thought to deal the death-stroke at a blow,
    To give all, once for all, but nevermore; –
    Then sit to hear the low waves fret the shore,
        Or watch the silent snow.

'Oh rest,' I thought, 'in silence and the dark;
    Oh rest, if nothing else, from head to feet:
    Though I may see no more the poppied wheat,
        Or sunny soaring lark.

'These chimes are slow, but surely strike at last;
    This sand is slow, but surely droppeth thro';
And much there is to suffer, much to do,
        Before the time be past.

'So will I labour, but will not rejoice:
    Will do and bear, but will not hope again;
Gone dead alike to pulses of quick pain,
        And pleasure's counterpoise:'

I said so in my heart, and so I thought
        My life would lapse, a tedious monotone:
I thought to shut myself, and dwell alone
        Unseeking and unsought.

But first I tired, and then my care grew slack;
        Till my heart slumbered, may-be wandered too: –
I felt the sunshine glow again, and knew
        The swallow on its track;

All birds awoke to building in the leaves,
        All buds awake to fullness and sweet scent,
Ah, too, my heart woke unawares, intent
        On fruitful harvest sheaves.

Full pulse of life, that I had deemed was dead,
        Full of throb of youth, that I had deemed at rest, –
Alas, I cannot build myself a nest,
        I cannot crown my head

With royal purple blossoms for the feast,
        Nor flush with laughter, nor exult in song; –
These joys may drift, as time now drifts along;
        And cease, as once they ceased.

I may pursue, and yet may not attain,
        Athirst and panting all the days I live:
Or seem to hold, yet nerve myself to give
        What once I gave, again.

THE HOUR AND THE GHOST (1856)

BRIDE
O love, love, hold me fast,
He draws me away from thee;
I cannot stem the blast,
Nor the cold strong sea:
Far away a light shines
Beyond the hills and pines;
It is lit for me.

BRIDEGROOM
I have thee close, my dear,
No terror can come near;
Only far off the northern light shines clear.

GHOST
Come with me, fair and false,
To our home, come home.
It is my voice that calls:
Once thou wast not afraid
When I woo'd, and said,
'Come, our nest is newly made'—
Now cross the tossing foam.

BRIDE
Hold me one moment longer,
He taunts me with the past,
His clutch is waxing stronger,

Hold me fast, hold me fast.
He draws me from thy heart,
And I cannot withhold:
He bids my spirit depart
With him into the cold: –
Oh bitter vows of old!

BRIDEGROOM
Lean on me, hide thine eyes:
Only ourselves, earth and skies,
Are present here: be wise.

GHOST
Lean on me, come away,
I will guide and steady:
Come, for I will not stay:
Come, for house and bed are ready.
Ah, sure bed and house,
For better and worse, for life and death:
Goal won with shortened breath:
Come, crown our vows.

BRIDE
One moment, one more word,
While my heart beats still,
While my breath is stirred
By my fainting will.
O friend, forsake me not,
Forget not as I forgot:

But keep thy heart for me,
Keep thy faith true and bright;
Thro' the lone cold winter night
Perhaps I may come to thee.

BRIDEGROOM
Nay peace, my darling, peace:
Let these dreams and terrors cease:
Who spoke of death or change or aught but ease?

GHOST
O fair frail sin,
O poor harvest gathered in!
Thou shalt visit him again
To watch his heart grow cold;
To know the gnawing pain
I knew of old;
To see one much more fair
Fill up the vacant chair,
Fill his heart, his children bear:—
While thou and I together
In the outcast weather
Toss and howl and spin.

A BETTER RESURRECTION (1857)

I have no wit, no words, no tears;
My heart within me like a stone
Is numbed too much for hopes or fears;
Look right, look left, I dwell alone;
I lift mine eyes, but dimmed with grief
No everlasting hills I see;
My life is in the falling leaf:
O Jesus, quicken me.

My life is like a faded leaf,
My harvest dwindled to a husk:
Truly my life is void and brief
And tedious in the barren dusk;
My life is like a frozen thing,
No bud nor greenness can I see:
Yet rise it shall – the sap of Spring;
O Jesus, rise in me.

My life is like a broken bowl,
A broken bowl that cannot hold
One drop of water for my soul
Or cordial in the searching cold;
Cast in the fire the perished thing,
Melt and remould it, till it be
A royal cup for Him, my King:
O Jesus, drink of me.

ADVENT (1858)

This Advent moon shines cold and clear,
    These Advent nights are long;
Our lamps have burned year after year,
    And still their flame is strong.
'Watchman, what of the night?' we cry,
    Heart-sick with hope deferred:
'No speaking signs are in the sky,'
    Is still the watchman's word.

The Porter watches at the gate,
    The servants watch within;
The watch is long betimes and late,
    The prize is slow to win.
'Watchman, what of the night?' but still
    His answer sounds the same:
'No daybreak tops the utmost hill,
    Nor pale our lamps of flame.'

One to another hear them speak,
    The patient virgins wise:
'Surely He is not far to seek,' –
    'All night we watch and rise.'
'The days are evil looking back,
    The coming days are dim;
Yet count we not His promise slack,
    But watch and wait for Him.'

One with another, soul with soul,
　　They kindle fire from fire:
'Friends watch us who have touched the goal.'
　　'They urge us, come up higher.'
'With them shall rest our waysore feet,
　　With them is built our home,
With Christ.' – 'They sweet, but He most sweet,
　　Sweeter than honeycomb.'

There no more parting, no more pain,
　　The distant ones brought near,
The lost so long are found again,
　　Long lost but longer dear:
Eye hath not seen, ear hath not heard,
　　Nor heart conceived that rest,
With them our good things long deferred,
　　With Jesus Christ our Best.

We weep because the night is long,
　　We laugh, for day shall rise,
We sing a slow contented song
　　And knock at Paradise.
Weeping we hold Him fast, Who wept
　　For us, we hold Him fast;
And will not let Him go except
　　He bless us first or last.

Weeping we hold Him fast to-night;
　　We will not let Him go
Till daybreak smite our wearied sight,

And summer smite the snow:
Then figs shall bud, and dove with dove
    Shall coo the livelong day;
Then He shall say, 'Arise, My love,
    My fair one, come away.'

BY THE SEA (1858)

Why does the sea moan evermore?
   Shut out from heaven it makes its moan,
It frets against the boundary shore;
   All earth's full rivers cannot fill
   The sea, that drinking thirsteth still.

Sheer miracles of loveliness
   Lie hid in its unlooked-on bed:
Anemones, salt, passionless,
   Blow flower-like; just enough alive
   To blow and multiply and thrive.

Shells quaint with curve, or spot, or spike,
   Encrusted live things argus-eyed,
All fair alike, yet all unlike,
   Are born without a pang, and die
   Without a pang, and so pass by.

WINTER RAIN (1859)

Every valley drinks,
    Every dell and hollow:
Where the kind rain sinks and sinks,
    Green of Spring will follow.

Yet a lapse of weeks
    Buds will burst their edges,
Strip their wool-coats, glue-coats, streaks,
    In the woods and hedges;

Weave a bower of love
    For birds to meet each other,
Weave a canopy above
    Nest and egg and mother.

But for fattening rain
    We should have no flowers,
Never a bud or leaf again
    But for soaking showers;

Never a mated bird
    In the rocking tree-tops,
Never indeed a flock or herd
    To graze upon the lea-crops.

Lambs so woolly white,
    Sheep the sun-bright leas on,
They could have no grass to bite
    But for rain in season.

We should find no moss
    In the shadiest places,
Find no waving meadow-grass
    Pied with broad-eyed daisies;

But miles of barren sand,
    With never a son or daughter,
Not a lily on the land,
    Or lily on the water.

THE LAMBS OF GRASMERE (1860)

The upland flocks grew starved and thinned:
    Their shepherds scarce could feed the lambs
Whose milkless mothers butted them,
    Or who were orphaned of their dams.
The lambs athirst for mother's milk
    Filled all the place with piteous sounds:
Their mothers' bones made white for miles
    The pastureless wet pasture grounds.

Day after day, night after night,
    From lamb to lamb the shepherds went,
With teapots for the bleating mouths
    Instead of nature's nourishment.
The little shivering gaping things
    Soon knew the step that brought them aid,
And fondled the protecting hand,
    And rubbed it with a woolly head.

Then, as the days waxed on to weeks,
    It was a pretty sight to see
These lambs with frisky heads and tails
    Skipping and leaping on the lea,
Bleating in tender, trustful tones,
    Resting on rocky crag or mound,
And following the beloved feet
    That once had sought for them and found.

These very shepherds of their flocks,
    These loving lambs so meek to please,
Are worthy of recording words
    And honour in their due degrees:
So I might live a hundred years,
    And roam from strand to foreign strand,
Yet not forget this flooded spring
    And scarce-saved lambs of Westmoreland.

AMOR MUNDI (1865)

'Oh where are you going with your love-locks flowing
    On the west wind blowing along this valley track?'
'The downhill path is easy, come with me an it please ye,
    We shall escape the uphill by never turning back.'

So they two went together in glowing August weather,
    The honey-breathing heather lay to their left and right;
And dear she was to dote on, her swift feet seemed to float on
    The air like soft twin pigeons too sportive to alight.

'Oh what is that in heaven where gray cloud-flakes are seven,
    Where blackest clouds hang riven just at the rainy skirt?'
'Oh that's a meteor sent us, a message dumb, portentous,
    An undeciphered solemn signal of help or hurt.'

'Oh what is that glides quickly where velvet flowers grow thickly,
    Their scent comes rich and sickly?' – 'A scaled and hooded
        worm.'
'Oh what's that in the hollow, so pale I quake to follow?'
    'Oh that's a thin dead body which waits the eternal term.'

'Turn again, O my sweetest, – turn again, false and fleetest:
    This beaten way thou beatest I fear is hell's own track.'
'Nay, too steep for hill-mounting; nay, too late for cost-counting:
    This downhill path is easy, but there's no turning back.'

MEMORY (1857)

I

I nursed it in my bosom while it lived,
    I hid it in my heart when it was dead;
In joy I sat alone, even so I grieved
    Alone and nothing said.

I shut the door to face the naked truth,
    I stood alone — I faced the truth alone,
Stripped bare of self-regard or forms or ruth
    Till first and last were shown.

I took the perfect balances and weighed;
    No shaking of my hand disturbed the poise;
Weighed, found it wanting: not a word I said,
    But silent made my choice.

None know the choice I made; I make it still.
    None know the choice I made and broke my heart,
Breaking mine idol: I have braced my will
    Once, chosen for once my part.

I broke it at a blow, I laid it cold,
    Crushed in my deep heart where it used to live.
My heart dies inch by inch; the time grows old,
    Grows old in which I grieve.

II (1865)

I have a room where into no one enters
   Save I myself alone:
   There sits a blessed memory on a throne,
There my life centres;

While winter comes and goes – oh tedious comer! –
   And while its nip-wind blows;
   While bloom the bloodless lilly and warm rose
Of lavish summer.

If any should force entrance he might see there
   One buried yet not dead,
Before whose face I no more bow my head
    Or bend my knee there;

But often in my worn life's autumn weather
   I watch there with clear eyes,
And think how it will be in Paradise
    When we're together.

'THEY DESIRE A BETTER COUNTRY' (1869)

I

I would not if I could undo my past,
  Tho' for its sake my future is a blank;
  My past, for which I have myself to thank,
For all its faults and follies first and last.
I would not cast anew the lot once cast,
  Or launch a second ship for one that sank,
  Or drug with sweets the bitterness I drank,
Or break by feasting my perpetual fast.
I would not if I could: for much more dear
  Is one remembrance than a hundred joys,
    More than a thousand hopes in jubilee;
  Dearer the music of one tearful voice
    That unforgotten calls and calls to me,
'Follow me here, rise up, and follow here.'

II

What seekest thou far in the unknown land?
  In hope I follow joy gone on before,
  In hope and fear persistent more and more,
As the dry desert lengthens out its sand.
Whilst day and night I carry in my hand
  The golden key to ope the golden door
  Of golden home; yet mine eye weepeth sore

For the long journey that must make no stand.
And who is this that veiled doth walk with thee?
    Lo, this is Love that walketh at my right;
        One exile holds us both, and we are bound
    To selfsame home-joys in the land of light.
Weeping thou walkest with him; weepeth he? –
        Some sobbing weep, some weep and make no sound.

III

A dimness of a glory glimmers here
    Thro' veils and distance from the space remote,
    A faintest far vibration of a note
Reaches to us and seems to bring us near,
Causing our face to glow with braver cheer,
    Making the serried mist to stand afloat,
    Subduing langour with an antidote,
And strengthening love almost to cast out fear,
Till for one moment golden city walls
    Rise looming on us, golden walls of home,
Light of our eyes until the darkness falls;
    Then thro' the outer darkness burdensome
I hear again the tender voice that calls,
    'Follow me hither, follow, rise, and come.'

MONNA INNOMINATA (circa 1881)

[Space here does not allow what Christina insisted on – that her sequence of fourteen sonnets, most probably written for Charles Cayley, be always printed together. This sampling should entice readers to read the entire sequence on the Internet, and thus experience it as intended.]

2

> *Era già 1'ora che volge il desio.* – Dante
>
> *Ricorro al tempo ch'io vi vidi prima.* – Petrarca

I wish I could remember that first day,
    First hour, first moment of your meeting me,
    If bright or dim the season, it might be
Summer or winter for aught I can say;
So unrecorded did it slip away,
    So blind was I to see and to foresee,
    So dull to mark the budding of my tree
That would not blossom yet for many a May.
If only I could recollect it, such
    A day of days! I let it come and go
    As traceless as a thaw of bygone snow;
It seemed to mean so little, meant so much;
If only now I could recall that touch,
    First touch of hand in hand – Did one but know!

8

Come dicesse a Dio: D'altro non calme. – Dante

Spero trovar pietà non che perdono. – Petrarca

'I, if I perish, perish' – Esther spake:
   And bride of life or death she made her fair
   In all the lustre of her perfum'd hair
And smiles that kindle longing but to slake.
She put on pomp of loveliness, to take
   Her husband thro' his eyes at unaware;
   She spread abroad her beauty for a snare,
Harmless as doves and subtle as a snake.
She trapp'd him with one mesh of silken hair,
   She vanquished him by wisdom of her wit,
      And built her people's house that it should stand: –
      If I might take my life so in my hand,
And for my love to Love put up my prayer,
And for love's sake by Love be granted it!

14

E la Sua Volontade è nostra pace. – Dante

Sol con questi pensier, con altre chiome. – Petrarca

Youth gone, and beauty gone if ever there
   Dwelt beauty in so poor a face as this;
   Youth gone and beauty, what remains of bliss?
I will not bind fresh roses in my hair,
To shame a cheek at best but little fair, –

Leave youth his roses, who can bear a thorn, –
I will not seek for blossoms anywhere,
 Except such common flowers as blow with corn.
Youth gone and beauty gone, what doth remain?
 The longing of a heart pent up forlorn,
  A silent heart whose silence loves and longs;
  The silence of a heart which sang its songs
 While youth and beauty made a summer morn,
Silence of love that cannot sing again.

RESURGAM (circa 1882)

From depth to height, from height to loftier height,
    The climber sets his foot and sets his face,
    Tracks lingering sunbeams to their halting-place,
And counts the last pulsations of the light.
Strenuous thro' day and unsurprised by night
    He runs a race with Time and wins the race,
    Emptied and stripped of all save only Grace,
Will, Love, a threefold panoply of might.
Darkness descends for light he toiled to seek;
    He stumbles on the darkened mountain-head,
    Left breathless in the unbreathable thin air,
    Made freeman of the living and the dead: –
He wots not he has topped the topmost peak,
    But the returning sun will find him there.

SON, REMEMBER (1889)

I laid beside thy gate, am Lazarus;
See me or see me not I still am there,
Hungry and thirsty, sore and sick and bare,
Dog-comforted and crumbs-solicitous:
While thou in all thy ways art sumptuous,
Daintily clothed, with dainties for thy fare:
Thus a world's wonder thou art quit of care,
And be I seen or not seen I am thus.
One day a worm for thee, a worm for me:
With my worm angel songs and trumpet burst
And plenitude an end of all desire:
But what for thee, alas! but what for thee?
Fire and an unextinguishable thirst,
Thirst in an unextinguishable fire.

AN ECHO FROM WILLOWWOOD (1890)

'O ye, all ye that walk in Willowwood.' – D.G. Rossetti

Two gazed into a pool, he gazed and she,
    Not hand in hand, yet heart in heart, I think,
    Pale and reluctant on the water's brink,
As on the brink of parting which must be.
Each eyed the other's aspect, she and he,
    Each felt one hungering heart leap up and sink,
    Each tasted bitterness which both must drink,
There on the brink of life's dividing sea.
Lilies upon the surface, deep below
    Two wistful faces craving each for each,
        Resolute and reluctant without speech: –
A sudden ripple made the faces flow
    One moment joined, to vanish out of reach:
So those hearts joined, and ah! were parted so.

BROTHER BRUIN (no date)

A dancing Bear grotesque and funny
Earned for his master heaps of money,
Gruff yet good-natured, fond of honey,
And cheerful if the day was sunny.
Past hedge and ditch, past pond and wood
He tramped, and on some common stood;
There, cottage children circling gaily,
He in their midmost footed daily.
Pandean pipes and drum and muzzle
Were quite enough his brain to puzzle:
But like a philosophic bear
He let alone extraneous care
And danced contented anywhere.

Still, year on year, and wear and tear,
Age even the gruffest, bluffest bear.
A day came when he scarce could prance,
And when his master looked askance
On dancing Bear who would not dance.

To looks succeeded blows; hard blows
Battered his ears and poor old nose.
From bluff and gruff he waxed curmudgeon;
He danced indeed, but danced in dudgeon,
Capered in fury fast and faster.
Ah, could he once but hug his master
And perish in one joint disaster!
But deafness, blindness, weakness growing,

Not fury's self could keep him going.
One dark day when the snow was snowing
His cup was brimmed to overflowing:
He tottered, toppled on one side,
Growled once, and shook his head, and died.
The master kicked and struck in vain,
The weary drudge had distanced pain
And never now would wince again.
The master growled; he might have howled
Or coaxed, – that slave's last growl was growled.
So gnawed by rancor and chagrin
One thing remained: he sold the skin.

What next the man did is not worth
Your notice or my setting forth,
But hearken what befell at last.
His idle working days gone past,
And not one friend and not one penny
Stored up (if ever he had any
Friends; but his coppers had been many),
All doors stood shut against him but
The workhouse door, which cannot shut.
There he droned on, – a grim old sinner,
Toothless, and grumbling for his dinner,
Unpitied quite, uncared for much
(The rate-payers not favouring such),
Hungry and gaunt, with time to spare;
Perhaps the hungry, gaunt old Bear
Danced back, a haunting memory.
Indeed, I hope so, for you see

If once the hard old heart relented,
The hard old man may have repented.

(*Christina campaigned against cruelty to animals.)

EPILOGUE

Exploring Christina's poems is like setting forth into an ocean, various and deep, covered with the vast stretches of her heaven above.

If we look down through the translucent series of repeated cadences that rise and fall – iambs and trochees like endless waves and troughs – we see intriguing creations that keep leading us farther into the voyage.

We range over the depths of a person who loved but was never fulfilled, who sought to replace romantic love with Divine love, and who suffered greatly from illnesses, especially during her terrible end.

She had likely best solaced her self by the writing of these poems.

BIBLIOGRAPHY

Christina Rossetti: A Biographical and Critical Study
Mackenzie Bell (Thomas Burleigh, 1898) (University of
California, digitised by Microsoft, published by Andesite Press,
an imprint of Creative Media Partners)

Christina Rossetti: The Complete Poems
text by R.W. Crump notes and introduction by Betty S. Flowers
(Penguin Books, 2005)

This Long Pursuit: Reflections of a Romantic Biographer
Richard Holmes (Vintage Books Edition, 2018)

An article by Henri Jacottet in a Swiss review

A Choice of Christina Rossetti Verse
Selected with an introduction by Elizabeth Jennings
(Faber and Faber, 1970)

The Pre-Raphaelites and Their Circle
edited and with an introduction by Cecil Y. Lang (The
University of Chicago Press, second edition revised, 1975)

Christina Rossetti: Poetry in Art
edited by Susan Owens and Nicholas Tromans (Yale
University Press, 2018)